ISLAMIZATION

REFORMING CONTEMPORARY KNOWLEDGE

DR. 'ABDUL HAMID A. ABU SULAYMAN

Qadeem Press

Qadeem Press

Qadeem Press Edition
Breathing Life into Forgotten Pages
www.qadeempress.com

Reprinted by Qadeem Press in 2025

Find our titles on your favourite online bookstore using the keyword 'Qadeem Press'

Contents

THE AUTHOR

- Dr. ʿAbdul Ḥamīd Aḥmad Abū Sulaymān was born in Makkah 1355/1936.
- Rector of the International Islamic University (IIU), Malaysia, from 1408/1988 to the present.
- Chairman of the Board, trustee, former president, and founding member of the International Institute of Islamic Thought.
- BA Commerce, University of Cairo, 1378/1959. MA Political Science, University of Cairo, 1381/1963. PhD International Relations, University of Pennsylvania, 1393/1973.
- Secretary, State Planning Committee, Saudi Arabia, 1383–84/1963–64.
- Chairman, Department of Political Science at King Saud University, Riyadh, Saudi Arabia, 1402–04/1982–84.
- Founding member of the Association of Muslim Social Scientists (AMSS), 1392/1972, and its former president, 1405–07/1985–87.
- Secretary General of the World Assembly of Muslim Youth (WAMY), 1393–99/1973–79.
- Author of several articles and books on reforming the Ummah, including:
  Crisis in the Muslim Mind, The Islamic Theory of Economics:

Philosophy and Contemporary Means, and *Towards an Islamic Theory of International Relations*.

- Dr. AbūSulaymān has been instrumental in bringing about many international academic conferences and seminars.

The Occasional Papers Series

The publication program of the International Institute of Islamic Thought (IIIT) has already addressed important issues in the field of Islamic thought and the Islamization of knowledge. In this respect a number of books have already appeared in several languages under fifteen main series: *Accessing the Islamic Intellectual Heritage; Academic Dissertations; Concepts and Terminology; Human Development; Indices; Islamic Methodology; Islamization of Culture; Islamization of Knowledge; Issues in Contemporary Islamic Thought; Lectures; Occasional Papers; Perspectives on Islamic Thought; Reform Movements and Methodologies of Change; Research Monographs and Studies in the Islamization of Knowledge.*

The Occasional Papers series, published by the Institute's London Office, covers a number of research papers, articles, and lectures from the Institute's worldwide program as well as from Muslim scholars willing to make contributions. These are presented individually in the form of booklets that can be easily read or referred to. It is hoped that the booklets will reach students, scholars, and specialists as well as major sections of the world's Muslims alike in order to generate a fruitful debate on the vital issue of Islamization, and to create an awareness of the intellectual crisis in its various shapes and forms, while encouraging an active role in the proposed course of action and solution. This series is also translated into other languages.

The sixth paper in this series *Islamization: Reforming Contemporary Knowledge*, was first published in the American Journal of Islamic Social Sciences (AJISS) Vol. 2 No. 2 under the title "Islamization of Knowledge with Special Reference to Political Science."

The use of Islamic terminology in transliteration is a policy of the IIIT. Some of the terms used are untranslatable, while others are so important that the Institute felt that familiarity with them is necessary for a better understanding of Islamic issues. These terms have been footnoted once or sometimes explained briefly between brackets. All those which have not yet been accepted in Anglo-Saxon dictionaries are in italic. As many of these occur more than once, readers are advised to refer to the relevant footnotes whenever necessary.

When mentioning dates, the Islamic one comes first, separated from the Gregorian one by a slash. When an Islamic date is mentioned alone, it is followed by AH.

The translation of the Qur'an used in this series is that of 'Abdullah Yūsuf 'Alī (Amana Corporation, revised, 1989). However, we made changes to verses quoted from it whenever we deemed it necessary for the sake of elucidation and precision of meaning.

IIIT, London

1413/1994

Editors' Note

The paper briefly tabulates the wide-ranging problems besetting the universal nation of Islam today and perceives the crisis of thought to be the root cause of present affliction. This is tragically ironic, the paper argues, since a profound respect for reason and knowledge characterized early Islam and was responsible for its brilliant success. Later developments, however, caused a split resulting in the creation of two leaderships: political and intellectual, the former adopting harsh, repressive measures, and the latter responding with rigidity and entrenchment. Thus, the vigorous and insightful *ijtihad* of *al Khulafa' al Rashidūn*'s time was sealed up, giving way to an inane fondness in the culture for abstraction and a general erosion of bold, creative thinking.

An attempt to recapture the original vitality, which was ever concomitant with the high moral code of Islam, in order to address the amazingly complex, intertwined and flexional aspects of modern life, forms much of the argument of the paper. In the process, both past and contemporary trends are scrutinized, and major areas of debate delineated. Emphasized throughout is the need for reform and redefinition in areas like ijma', *ifta'*, and *qiyās*. This is also extended to such concepts as reason, knowledge, and education in relation to divine revelation. Fashionable and borrowed concepts like democracy and sovereignty are examined in the context of a considered Islamization of one discipline-that of political science.

I. The Crisis of Knowledge

This paper discusses the crisis of thought prevailing in the Muslim world today and considers it a fundamental cause of the current degeneration, decadence, and backwardness of the Ummah. It also highlights the potential role of the International Institute of Islamic Thought in counteracting and ultimately overcoming the crisis.

Such a theme inevitably brings the Islamic concept of knowledge to the forefront. First of all, it must be decided whether such an investigation is merely an intellectual extravaganza or whether there is actually a real issue that deserves investigation. No one possessing insight into the condition of the Ummah can fail to realize that there exists in it a crisis resulting from:

1. Backwardness;

2. All-pervasive weakness and lethargy;

3. Intellectual stagnation;

4. Absence of *ijtihad*[1];

---

[1] *ijtihad*: a creative but disciplined intellectual effort to derive legal rulings from those sources while taking into consideration the variables imposed by the fluctuating circumstances of Muslim society. For recent papers on the subject see: Tahä J. al 'Alwānī, "Taqlid and Ijtihad", AJISS, VIII, 1, pp. 129-142; "The Crisis in Fiqh and the Methodology of Ijtihad", VIII, 2, pp. 317-337; "Taqlid and the Stagnation of Muslim Mind," VIII, 3, pp. 513- 524; "Taqlid and Ijtihad," IX, 2, pp. 233-242; "The Scope of Taqlid," IX, 3, pp. 107-1 383-386, "The Crisis of Thought and *Ijtihad*", X, 2, pp. 234-237.

5. Absence of cultural progress; and

6. Estrangement from the basic norms of islamic civilization.

All these issues indicate, in one way or another, the intellectual crisis prevailing in the Muslim world. There is no doubt that this crisis is both cause and evidence of the decadence and impotence of the Ummah and prevents it from contributing decisively or even significantly let alone constructively to the culture and civilization of the modern world. This incapability is further exacerbated by the frequency of political, economic, and military crises.

Whether we discuss the problem of ijtihad in Islamic thought or the causes of the disparity between our past and present, the disparity between Islamic values and the actions of Muslims, or the insignificance and marginality of the presence of the Islamic character, we inevitably find that the crisis in the Ummah's conception of knowledge is the sole cause of the state of decadence of our Ummah. Removing its misconception is essential for any clarity of vision, effective reforms, and redirection of the Ummah.

It is a fact that despite its backwardness, the Ummah has never been short of natural resources, human potentiality, or historical perspective. Nor has it been deficient in ethical and moral values. It still possesses the time-honoured principles and values revealed in the Qur'an and contained in the Hadith. Furthermore, the Ummah has made limited and short-lived attempts in Morocco, the Sudan, the Arabian Peninsula, the Indian subcontinent, and other Muslim countries to salvage itself from its decadent and backward situation by reviving the perspectives envisaged by traditional thinking. But all those attempts have been confined largely to Muslims in remote desert and rural areas. They have failed to influence or attract the urban population. They have failed to counter the distracted and diseased forces of the metropolitan cities which are hostile to the cultural, intellectual, and organizational progress of the Ummah and evidence of its impotence.

Whenever the Ummah has tried to adopt foreign tactics, it has undergone bitter experiences, such as those which took place in Turkey during the reign of Sultan Salīm III and in Egypt ever since the reign of Muhammad 'Alī. The Turkish experience is the oldest and the most comprehensive. These countries tried to imitate the technical, organizational, and intellectual styles of foreign countries, basing their political constitutions on concepts such as nationalism and secularism, which they imposed through state intervention. But the imitative experiments have ended in miserable failures, as can be seen in extremity by the utter helplessness and deteriorating conditions of modern Egypt and Turkey.

This leads us to the obvious conclusion that the imitation of foreign styles is just as fruitless as the traditional imitation of past perspectives. Both of them have failed to achieve the Ummah's objectives. It is imperative that reconstruction require an original redefining of the intellectual and socio-cultural potentialities of the Ummah on the basis of its values, principles, and historical perspectives. A redefinition of knowledge should be the starting point for such a reconstruction.

A. How the Crisis of Knowledge Began

We must realize that knowledge was the basic cause of the progress and development of the Ummah. At its very beginning, Islam managed to build up the structure and character of the Ummah on the firm basis of knowledge acquired through its proper sources, namely, divine revelation and active reason. Divine guidance endowed Prophet Muhammad (SAAS)[2] with a clarity of vision that enabled him to weave an exemplary pattern of life. The Qur'an explicitly encourages the gaining of knowledge and education as well as the value of learning from experience. The first revelation calls upon the Prophet and humanity to seek education and acquire knowledge in accordance with the divine guidance:

> Read [and understand] in the Name of thy Lord and Cherisher (Qur'an 96:1)

There was nobody more capable of leadership than Prophet Muhammad. Nonetheless, he used to consult his companions on almost all matters, and this enabled him to excel in directing the individual and collective affairs of the Muslims in the most efficient and comprehensive manner during war and peace. The extent of that strength can be gauged by the failure of the West to counter the challenge of the 'Uthmānīyūn (the Ottomans) until it started the intellectual and cultural revolution that came to be known as the Age of Enlightenment. Through that enlightenment, the Western

---

[2] SAAS-*Salla Allahu 'Alayhi wa Sallam*: May the peace and blessing of Allah be upon him; said whenever the name of the Prophet Muhammad is mentioned, or whenever he is referred to as the Prophet of God.

nations reorganized their forces, defeated the Muslims, and emerged as a formidable factor in history.

On the other hand, when the tables had turned and the balance of power had shifted to the West, the reaction of the Muslims, which was essentially political and military, failed to make use of a spirit of sacrifice and sincerity which would have enabled them to defend not only their homeland but their values as well. Backward and lacking confidence in its moral and spiritual values, the Ummah attempted to counter Western power, but this resulted only in bloodshed, economic disorder, and general deterioration in every walk of life. An analysis of the relations between any two Muslim countries reveals tendencies which sabotage the overall interests of Muslims.

With the passage of time, knowledge deteriorated, and the Islamic character weakened. In short, there followed a steady decline in the cultural and intellectual domain, despite the fact that the spirit of sacrifice and sincerity persisted in devout Muslims. Virtues and qualities, such as competence, energy, initiative, seriousness, creativity, and wisdom, which had characterized the early "emergency" phase of the Ummah and which had enabled the Muslims not only to defeat the forces of anarchy, disruption, and barbarism but also to win for them respect and admiration all over the world, have disappeared. One wonders why the virtues that enabled the Muslims to establish a matchless civilization have disappeared; why the energy and resourcefulness have been dissipated; why the Islamic character has degenerated; and how it is that the whole Islamic system has disintegrated.

B. The Split in Leadership

The strength of the Ummah resided in the *khilafah*[3] system established by the Prophet in Madīnah. But during the process of local defence and outside conquest, tribal men infiltrated the army. The habits of thought and upbringing of these men were far below the standard of the Companions (RAA)[4] who had built the state in Madīnah. Lacking the spirit that motivated the *khulafa'*, these tribal men sought to secure their position by establishing a new system which was a mixture of the tribal notions prevailing in the pre-Islamic state of ignorance and the half-cherished Islamic notions acquired after the rise of Islam. That hybrid system was the starting point of the deterioration and ultimate disintegration.

Although the ruling body was guided by tribal norms, the people in the Hijaz, who represented the true Islamic consciousness, refused to accept the new tribal order and revolted against it using physical force. This encounter led to a series of internal wars led by a number of pious personalities such as al Husayn ibn 'Alī, 'Abd Allah ibn al Zubayr, Zayd ibn 'Alī, and others.

But the spirit of revolt remained confined to the Hijaz for two reasons. First of all, the newly converted Muslim populace was not well acquainted with the teachings of Islam. Second, as more and more people embraced Islam, they brought with them their traditional pre-Islamic customs and habits. Furthermore, a separation between religion and politics gradually isolated the

---

[3] *khilafah*: The institution of man as vicegerent of Allah (sing. khalifah, pl. *khulafa'*).

[4] RAA-*Radiya Allahu 'Anhu/'Anha* (or *'Anhum*): May Allah be pleased with him/her (or with them). Said whenever a Companion of the Prophet is mentioned by name.

intellectual leadership. The religious scholars, who always represented the opposition to the political authorities, were forced to withdraw as far as possible from the scuffles and struggles of politics. Thus, Imam Abū Hanīfah died in prison refusing to accept a high judicial post. Imam Malik ibn Anas was physically tortured because he gave a verdict on compulsory divorce against the wishes of the rulers. Imām al Shafi'i was forced to emigrate from Baghdad to Egypt.

This schism of the intellectual and political leadership initiated the evils of deceit, ignorance, and arrogance which crippled the structure of the Ummah. Religious thought was confined to the level of abstraction and was not allowed to function in regulating practice and evaluating experience and experiment. Thus, the very concept of the Ummah and its leadership began to wither.

This withering was accelerated by the theoretical and unsystematic manner of Islamic thinking, which made the Ummah lose touch with its attitudes, needs, and priorities for progress. On the other hand, the deviation of the political leadership and the measures it adopted to silence all opposition made the task of the intellectual leaders more difficult than ever before. Mutual distrust was the rule rather than the exception. The religious personalities became suspicious and skeptical of any initiative taken by the politicians, irrespective of its validity. This skepticism created an uncompromising attitude in the intellectual leadership, a rigidity that sealed up the avenues of ijtihad in an attempt to protect the teachings ordained in the Qur'an and the Hadith from any deviations threatening their authenticity. Such a rigidity is understandable, but it must be admitted that the intellectual leaders failed to foresee the dangers of confining and concentrating their efforts on abstract thinking.

There was another conflict regarding the application of the teachings of Islam in everyday life. This conflict impoverished the intellectual activities of the Muslims and consequently enfeebled the character of Muslim culture and civilization. During the early days of Islam, Islamic ideology was marked by a spirit of initiative, fruitful interaction, resourcefulness, competence, and Vigor. It was a time that fostered intellectual courage and moral uprightness. That quality kept the spirit of Islam fully alive, its aims and objectives clearly defined, expounded, and pronounced. A conflict started as early as the time of Abu Bakr, when he clarified the misconceptions lurking in the heads of the tribal men who had embraced Islam. On the basis of that clarification, Abū Bakr obliged the tribal men to pay *zakah*[5] and pledge allegiance to the khalifah. Similarly, 'Umar resorted to ijtihad in order to clarify issues regarding *kharaj*[6] and divorce. So did 'Alī ibn Abū Tālib on various issues. Admittedly, the period of the first four *khulafa'* (al *Khulafa' al Rashidūn*) was a natural continuation of the time of the Prophet. Nonetheless, many aspects of their era, especially in the field of administration, clearly indicate their depth of insight into, and

---

[5] *zakah*: Usually rendered as the poor-due' or legal charity, *zakah* is the obligatory sharing of wealth with the poor and the community at the annual rate of 2.5% of appropriated wealth above a certain minimum.

[6] *Kharaj*: land tax.

strict adherence to, the *Shari'ah*[7] to settle the problems they encountered.

The phenomenon of technical, abstract, and academic intellectuality was not known then. It emerged alarmingly when the gulf widened between the intellectual and political leadership. It is no wonder that this tendency dealt a blow to the true spirit of Islamic legislation and politics. With the passage of time, Islamic thought became lifeless.

During the reign of the first four *khulafa'*, the leaders struck a harmonious balance between religion and politics. The *khulafa's* faith and practices fully adhered to Islamic values and objectives and consequently won the confidence of their subjects. The fruits of their experience and thought were utilized for the welfare of the Ummah. There was no dichotomy or conflict between the temporal and the spiritual. The *khulafa'* firmly believed that human reason was fallible but could be utilized within the limits set by divine revelation.

But when the leadership lost its strength, the gulf between religion and politics widened, and there followed more and more dependence upon reason. At the same time, the Muslims' conquest of other nations and the contact resulting therefrom brought about an intellectual and cultural pomposity which lacked seriousness, especially in the court and political circles. As a result, academic pursuits did not adhere strictly to the spirit and objectives of Islam. This tendency made itself conspicuously evident in the popularity

---

[7] *Shari'ah*: The collective name for all the laws of Islam, including Islam's whole religious and liturgical, ethical and jurisprudential systems.

of rhetoric, philosophical and theological discussions, and sophistry. Those in authority made the situation even worse by patronizing philosophers, orators, and fictioners. Such unwholesome favoritism led to the emergence of extremist movements such as the *Ikhwan al Safa*[8], the *Batiniyah*[9], and the Sophists.

It goes without saying that these intellectual pursuits were not governed by the spirit of Islam. The clearest instance was the indulgence in discussing the nature of God's transcendence. Such a theme has no place in Islamic thought because the Qur'an explicitly pronounces:

> He [Allah] begets not, nor is He begotten. and there is none like unto Him. (112: 3-4)

The heretical nature of the futile and unbridled rationalism of the age outraged eminent Muslim scholars such as al Ghazali and Ibn Taymiyah, who spent their lives exposing the deviations introduced by these sects.

The struggle against the infiltration of foreign thought and culture proved fruitless, and as a result, Muslim scholars grew more and more skeptical and hostile toward the manifestations of reason in philosophical discourse. Henceforth academic pursuits became more inclined toward explicating the *Shari'ah* texts, the Arabic language, and jurisprudence. This tendency led to more concentration on second-rate thought, authentication of texts, and the compiling of glossaries and historical trivialities. The result was

---

8 Brotherhood of *Safa*: Brethren of Purity.

9 *Batiniyah*: Those who believe in divining a hidden meaning in the revealed text.

a state of intellectual incompetence which closed off the gates of ijtihad and promoted concentration on textual studies in a repetitious way and from an exclusively theoretical point of view.

II. The Present Crisis in Islamic Thought

The present crisis in Islamic thought is more alarming than ever before. Admittedly, the long-standing isolation previously mentioned has resulted in incompetence and superficiality of thought, but it is not the main cause of the crisis. Much more to the point is the inability of our thinkers to measure the extent of change that has taken place in the realm of knowledge, culture, and civilization in the modern world. There is also a parallel inability to locate the points of strength in the sources of Islamic knowledge and to learn from past experience.

As a result of this situation, people have felt the urgent need to restore ijtihad. This call has brought about conflicting reactions. Some have argued that it should be restored even if it has been revoked. Nonetheless, ijtihad has remained sealed up, and consequently, thought has remained inept. Here and there, however, occasional glimpses of systematic thought have emerged which could have defined the direction of knowledge, thought, and culture but which have failed to mature into proper schools of thought because they depended so heavily upon the characters of the men who initiated them.

But the redefinition and redirection of thought require a radical change in our attitude toward what the human mind can and cannot do. This is essential, because the main cause of the crisis of knowledge lies in the way we understand knowledge, which has confused our attitude toward reason. The crisis also lies in the nature of our Islamic methods of research, which are confined to textual studies of language, traditions, and orthodox jurisprudence. These two attitudes are manifested in our tendency to regard the *faqih*[10] as one who is still capable of resolving the crisis of thought, culture, and knowledge. The jurist is expected to use ijtihad in order to provide solutions and alternatives which the Ummah might use to counter its enemies.

If we desire to reform our knowledge, culture, and civilization in order to steer the Islamic movement in the right direction, to invigorate the Muslim character, and to formulate plans for Islamic *da'wah*[11], we must initiate reform in each of the following ways:

First, we must rectify the relationship between divine revelation and reason as manifested in our lines of thinking.

Second, we must redefine knowledge in a way that leaves no ambiguity about concepts such as ijtihad and roles such as that of the *faqih*. In this respect, there must be a clear-cut distinction drawn between ijtihad and *ifta*[12] in the light of the current trends in Islamic thought.

Third, we must reorganize and reorient the methodology of Islamic education and instruction in order to put an end to the confused dualism that divides knowledge into intellectual, social,

---

[10] *faqih* (pl. *fuqaha*): Specialist in Islamic jurisprudence (*fiqh*). Faqih can be a synonym with *'alim* (pl. *ulama*) meaning Islamic scholar.

[11] da'wah: Call to Islam, preaching.

[12] *ifta*: Deliverance of formal legal opinion.

religious, and legal categories, thereby creating further dualism in the leadership.

A. Rectifying the Relationship between Revelation and Reason

It is quite obvious that the position of superiority achieved by the West in the realm of knowledge and thought is purely intellectual and has nothing to do with divine revelation. In spite of the tremendous achievements reached by Western thought in experimental fields, Western scholars cannot deny the maladjustment and imbalance in Western society. This is caused by the inapplicability of empirical methods to the conflict between societal welfare on the one hand and the pursuance of personal desires and interests on the other. This is so because human reason alone is incapable of attaining the ultimate truth about and full understanding of what is desirable for humanity in this life and in the life hereafter. This predicament lies in the fact that Western civilization is lost in so many haphazard and contradictory theories that it is unable to arrive at one single theory or confidently resolve any problem. Islamic sources of knowledge, on the other hand, are divine revelation and reason. There is no problem in saying that revelation and reason are the sources of knowledge in Islam, but the problem lies in defining and giving a concrete shape to the relationship between the two.

Such a dichotomy has no place in Islam, because divine revelation embodies the objectives of human reason and prescribes checks and controls against intellectual deviation and spiritual perversion. Nonetheless, it is important for Muslims to realize that divine revelation itself might be subject to misunderstanding and misinterpretation. This is both a problem and a challenge which Muslims have to face, because an inadequate use of intellectual faculties may also thwart the revelation itself. Fears about the negative results of a perverted misuse of intellectual faculties, which have beset the lives of non-Muslims, should not discourage Muslims from the application of reason. Should that be the case, Muslims would lose the golden opportunity that divine revelation offers in defining the role of the mind for pursuing the purpose of existence. They might also misunderstand divine revelation, thereby wreaking further damage.

One can cite countless examples of the Ummah's practices that result from ignorance, inexperience, and a failure to use systematic reasoning. Such deficiencies not infrequently lead the *ulama*[13] to reach deceptive and unreasonable conclusions or to adopt unfortunate attitudes, which cause more harm than good and also alienate Muslims and non-Muslims alike from the cause of Allah (SWT)[14]. This is the reason why it has to be emphasized that the crisis lies in the perception of the relationship between revelation and reason. This is to say that the two should be harmoniously synchronized so that they are inextricably bound with one another, Revelation cannot function in the absence of a rational mind, and the rational mind is not worthy of recognition or respect if it strays from pure and simple revelation. Therefore, it can be concluded that the core of the problem does not lie in the failure to use the mental

---

[13] See note 10 above.

[14] SWT-*Subhanahu wa Ta'ala*: May He be praised and may His transcendence be affirmed. Said when referring to Allah.

faculties, but in the manner in which they are made to function as well as the quality of their functioning.

The mind is an indispensable source of knowledge, thought, and culture, but it must be used cautiously within the defined purpose of existence and the framework of revelation in a disciplined and committed spirit which seeks to enrich rather than enfeeble Islamic thought. In this way, we can avoid the haphazard practices and false assumptions that have disturbed and occasionally distorted our history.

This leads me to conclude with a few emphatic statements. It is un-Islamic to indulge in any investigation or express one's opinion on any matter if one is uncertain of one's knowledge in this regard. Ignorance cannot enlighten anything or anybody. Conclusions reached through ignorance are usually extravagant and excessive. Islam enjoins us to refrain from extravagance and excessiveness and requires us to exercise mercy and kindness. Accordingly, it is equally un-Islamic to disregard the needs of Muslims and the effect of what we say on their behavior. It is also un-Islamic to accept the notion that we are unable to look after the affairs of Muslims as a result of an inability to apply our mental faculties properly. Last but not least, it is un-Islamic to give reins and spurs to the human mind in total ignorance of Islamic principles, ideals, and values.

One example may clarify my point. If Muslim scholars had based their thinking solely on the apparent meaning of Islamic texts when considering the pricing system, they would have prohibited controlling prices. But common sense alerted them to the problems that might result. Observation and experience indicate quite clearly that in the absence of a truly free market, the absence of a pricing system creates vices such as exploitation, fraud, and injustice to the masses. That being the case, an absolute prohibition of a pricing system would undermine the cause of Islam, which preaches justice and equality. This shows that the mind has been used advantageously and has proved capable of giving proper guidance in the light of the total spirit of Islam. By realizing the priority of justice in Islam, it has not been distracted by technical theories and considerations from accepting a system that might put a minimum of checks and controls on economic transactions.

Unfortunately, those whose common sense directed them to the necessity of a pricing system failed to analyse and comprehend the phenomenon in its totality. More consideration should have been given to reconstructing the market and reforming the financial infrastructure to achieve balanced transactions. It was not enough to introduce protective measures and be content with them. Nonetheless, it has to be emphasized that such an introduction can reflect a courageous and well-informed policy. Such courage would demonstrate the good that can be derived from purposefully applying a seriously committed Islamic line of thinking to investigate a phenomenon and manage it cautiously and wisely within the framework of the fundamentals of Islam.

B. Redefining the Scope of Knowledge

One of the mistakes made by Muslim researchers as a result of the influence of historical practice upon their manner of thinking is their continued belief that the orthodox jurists are the only persons responsible for defining the scope of Islamic knowledge. They believe them to be capable of providing the thinking and ijtihad necessary for reorganizing modern life. They assume that the authority of these jurists can provide a basis for an active response to the challenges the Ummah faces and supply it with alternatives to counter hostile cultural and social interests.

This understanding is basically wrong, because it rests upon an assumption that is no longer valid in the realm of modern knowledge, namely that the *faqih* possesses the necessary knowledge capable of providing Islamic alternatives through rational effort. Historically, this understanding was largely true because the *faqih* was a merchant, philosopher, mathematician, physician, and chemist. In addition, he was well versed in various branches of Islamic Shari'ah and jurisprudence. In that capacity, he was well equipped to direct his versatile intellectual abilities in the service of Islamic studies and in the interest of the Ummah.

We must realize, however, that modern knowledge has expanded immensely and has become so complex that it is impossible for a single person to acquire a command of the multiple aspects of even one branch of knowledge. This means that the ability necessary for *ijtihad* in any one of the various branches of knowledge requires specialization in and absolute mastery of that branch. In view of this multifaceted knowledge and the multifariousness of the fields of specialization, it is clear that ijtihad, insights, solutions, and alternatives in the domain of social and scientific knowledge cannot be provided by the specialists in legal studies alone: the task and the expectation are impossible.

This is most noticeable in the case of legislators who formulate and categorize laws and regulations covering economics, politics, information, industry, and scientific research or transformation. It cannot be assumed that they are the masterminds of the knowledge from which the laws and regulations have been derived. In view of the achievements and progress made in the modern fields of knowledge, we need to bring to bear the expertise of economists, politicians, administrators, and others who are well versed in the various affairs of social life as well. Such specialists should at the same time have firsthand knowledge of the Qur'an and the Sunnah, which give them proper insight into the morals, values, and purpose of existence as understood by Islam and validate their activities and contributions.

Such well-equipped specialists can develop the legislative source materials on which legislators can draw to meet the day-to-day requirements of the Ummah and vitalize its existence. By so doing, we can define the place of *ifta'* and legislature in the field of knowledge as well as realistically assess their potential social performance in order to avoid overburdening or misguiding either the experts or the Solons. This means that we will continue to call upon orthodox jurists and legislators to provide the insights, originality, and answers to new, intricate problems, but only in conjunction with an unflinching determination to keep them abreast of knowledge by preparing cadres of specialists capable of living up to the expectations and requirements of the age.

The responsibility of these interdisciplinary specialist cadres should not remain confined to a particular legislative think-tank or authority, but should be shared by the academic community, representatives of interest groups, and legislative bodies responsible for pronouncements arising from the needs and demands of the Ummah's social structure. This approach is necessary to enhance the intellectual vitality of the Ummah and to reduce any ambiguities or anxieties in its daily practices.

C. Establishing an Islamic Infrastructure and Education

Historically, the dichotomy between the political and the intellectual leadership was the main cause of the weakness and gradual withering away of Islamic knowledge and culture, and also the increase in the tyranny, ignorance, and despotism of the politicians. At present, as a result of the historical vacuum created by that dichotomy and the military, political, and cultural impact of Western colonial influence, there is still a dualism in knowledge itself.

There exists a so-called Islamic knowledge, which until recently became limited in scope and legalistic in nature, so much so that some of the so-called Islamic states dominated by secularism have dared to amend, alter, and pervert even family and personal laws.

There also exists in the Muslim world an imported secular knowledge which dominates every aspect of life, and whose advocates respond thoughtlessly to and imitate blindly the trends and developments of the age. This secularism is perpetuated and popularized by institutions, universities, and organizations in various Islamic countries.

The two categories of knowledge form a tree which is unable to grow, because the first category lacks the essential dynamism to foster growth and the second is alien to the Muslims, their lands, goals, and objectives. For this reason, when one talks about reforming and reconstructing the perspectives of Islamic knowledge and culture, one has in mind the initiation of a revival that should make them fit once again for production and growth. But that goal cannot be achieved without reconstructing and reorienting the programs of education and instruction. The hope for and the possibility of uprooting the forms of dualism in knowledge at the leadership level lies in providing technically able and Islamically committed cadres who are well-versed in simplified and purposefully categorized Islamic teachings.

Initially, each field of specialization must include in its curriculum a sufficient number of texts of religious knowledge to mould and guide the mentality of the learner. Next, it is imperative that every aspect of the curriculum reflect the objectives and values of the teachings of Islam in a harmoniously comprehensive manner so as not to lose the essential unity of the nature of Islamic knowledge and culture. Only then can the Ummah claim to possess knowledge that corresponds to Islamic objectives. This approach will not leave any room for an Islamic university and a secular university to coexist at the same time and in the same place. There will be no room for limiting our objectives, thought, and curricula by confining them to legal and linguistic studies. There will be room only for studies oriented toward fulfilling the Islamic purpose of existence, abiding by its checks and controls, and following an Islamic approach to the sciences and the humanities. The reorientation of education and instruction toward a purely Islamic style for the fulfillment of Islamic objectives would include methodology, professional commitment, and social participation in accordance with what is proper for each field and is required by the Muslim Ummah.

Talking about the bases of reform necessarily leads to an investigation of the methods of research and foundations of Islamic thought in order to determine their place in the process of reform. This is necessary for a clear understanding of the relationship between the redefinition of knowledge and the reconstruction of its research methods on the one hand, and the historical concept of the foundations of Islamic thought and the terms associated with it on the other.

Generally speaking, the term *uşūl*[15] refers to the sources and research methods in Islamic thought. In view of what has already been said, it seems proper that the direction of reform should begin with investigating the sources of knowledge and determining the organic relationship between them prior to considering the issue of *usûl. Uşül* is an inclusive term comprising a variety of unrelated issues which historical circumstances caused to be grouped together. In my opinion, this lack of homogeneity has become a source of confused intellectual and methodological complications. The term stands for the Qur'an, the *Sunnah*, *qiyās,*[16] and *ijma. Ijma'* is a legal concept comprising the consensus of the competent scholars of the Ummah with regard to legal questions that are not addressed in the written sources. *Qiyās* is also one of the legitimate sources of

[15] *usül al fiqh*: science of Islamic jurisprudence, or the methodology of deriving laws from the sources of Islam and establishing their juristic or constitutional validity.

[16] *qiyās*: Logical deduction from the Qur'an and Sunnah as sources of Islamic law.

normative legal inference. Other elements of *uşūl* are *darūrah* (necessity), *maslahah* (need of the hour), *istishab*[17] and *istihsan*[18], all of which are methods of facilitating legal inference, i.e., the application of the Qur'an to practical problems. This framework requires an objective and patient study to trace the evolutionary development of the *usul*, or methodology of Islamic thought, and the various influences leading to its present formation in order to develop and invigorate it so that it can better serve Islamic knowledge, culture, and legislation.

In spite of the superficiality, inaccessibility, and general lack of specialized studies of the research methods from which thought originated in the early phase of Islam, it is quite easy for us to perceive the vitality, initiative, courage, and perspicuity that characterized the thinkers of that generation. At the same time, one cannot help noticing the instances of stagnation, rigidity, and trivialization that crept into Islamic research methods, particularly with regard to the concept of ijma' as understood by the exponents of *uşūl*.

It is important to realize that the current concept of *usûl* was formulated in an earlier period and, in that capacity, it responded to the needs of that age. The developments, changes, and trends in the realities of Muslim life require a reframing to determine the

---

[17] *istishab*: The continuation of an established law which has not been revoked or rescinded.

[18] *istihsan*: As source of Islamic law, the acceptance of a rule because of its superior equity in comparison with an already established law.

amendments that have to be introduced into the research methods pertaining to the study of revelation and the pursuit of knowledge.

While instituting reform, the factors of time and place have to be given adequate consideration with regard to the influence they might have on the interpretation or amendment of each text individually as well as on the totality of related texts within the framework of the principles of divine guidance. For example, the traditions of the Prophet and the books on jurisprudence speak in minute detail about the procedures pertaining to raising *zakah* on animal and plant production, because these were the sources of wealth in the Arabian Peninsula during the life of the Prophet. That is why he had to utilize whatever resources were available to meet the needs of the poor and indigent sections of the population. We also find instances of exemption from *zakah* in industry, mining, and estate property, in accordance with the level of wealth and production at that time. But at present we find that the wealth resulting from the production of oil is historically unprecedented, and that the future of revenues from estate property and that of the nation itself depends upon industry. Such developments require careful and focal reconsideration to achieve the noble objectives of meeting the needs of the indigent and the "have-nots."

The effects of time and place must influence our methodological approach to understanding the totality of the Sunnah of the Prophet and the comprehensiveness of the instructions and plans which enabled him to found and organize the true Islamic society.

Research work, particularly on the Sunnah of the Prophet, has to be developed on similar lines. What is required is a comprehensive and detailed study of the texts pertaining to a particular issue so as to establish the relationships between the various issues in the light of the objectives formulated by the Prophet for the Muslims in Madīnah and the Arabian Peninsula. A good example of such a fruitful approach was represented by a conference held by the Muslim Students Association of the United States and Canada.[19] The participants deliberated on the issue of usury, singling out and studying patiently every relevant text focusing on how the policies which the Prophet adopted and the goals which he set for the abolition of the system of usury show his wisdom and far-reaching insight. The deliberations brought to light some texts which were hitherto quite unknown and dispelled all ambiguities.

The effect of time and place and a comprehensive study of issues in their right perspective puts special emphasis on the method of *qiyās*, which ensures arriving at conclusions that are not limited by time and place but are in keeping with the spirit of the Prophet's Sunnah. In addition, *qiyas* will put an end to the continuous disputes in which partial and unrelated texts are advanced without any comprehensive vision of what the realities of the present time require. These disputes continue to tear the Ummah apart through the repetitious introduction of trivial issues. Furthermore, the failure of research to point out the damage to Islamic studies and the inefficiency which results from such

---

[19] The proceedings of the conference have been published in the form of a book entitled: *Contemporary Aspects of Economic and Social Thinking in Islam.*

trivialization points to the ineffectiveness of such disputes. It needs to be emphasized that, however valid a partial issue may be, it is not necessarily the real issue. On the contrary, the conclusions arrived at may well be the exact opposite of what might have been decided if the issue had been considered in its entirety, within the context of time and place, because such a holistic approach influences and highlights both the concept of *qiyas* itself as well as the validity of the purpose it is required to serve.

I place much hope in the reconsideration of our approach to revealed knowledge and the quest for acquired knowledge. The way to achieve this seems to lie in clarifying the role we give to the mind to investigate, discover, and verify subjects while giving due emphasis to the factors of time and place. Such reconsideration is the way to allow the mind to serve and be guided by revelation so that we may attain-through *qiyas*-a comprehensive vision with true insight into the core of our heritage, whose fundamentals and objectives are beyond the barriers of time and place. This approach will enable us to reconstruct our system of education and instruction and thereby achieve the unity of knowledge and leadership.

III. The Islamization of a Discipline: Political Science

The problems facing Islamic thought are complex, but they can be best illustrated by a consideration of a single discipline. First, political science is a social field of study which for various reasons has hitherto drawn little attention from Muslim scholars. Second, the historical dichotomy between the intellectual and political leadership has caused technical and unsystematic methods of thought to dominate Islamic studies. Thirdly, these inadequate methods have failed to develop a comprehensive vision capable of providing solutions and alternatives appropriate for the requirements of time and place to meet the challenges of progress, change, and construction.

A. Examples of Deficiency

The intellectual deficiency in this field may be illustrated by citing two examples. The questions raised here have already been posed by two eminent figures in the field of Islamic jurisprudence, but they remain unresolved because of the inadequacy of their methodology, which can be detected by any specialist in the field.

The first example comes from Ibn Rushd. In his treatise on Islamic jurisprudence, *Bidayat al Mujtahid wa Nihayah al Muqtasid*, this eminent scholar describes the differences of opinion among jurists over the sanctions against cutting trees in time of war. The confusion originated from the assumption that Abū Bakr's prohibition against cutting trees during the *riddah*[20] wars was not in conformity with the Sunnah of the Prophet, who, during his campaign against Banü al Nadīr, burnt down their date trees. To reach a compromise for the justification of Abu Bakr's action, it is argued that: a) Abū Bakr knew that the permission to burn trees was later abrogated by the Prophet, and b) the Prophet's action was confined to the particular campaign against Banü al Nadir. Ibn Rushd's final comment on the literature regarding this issue is that "those who endorse the Prophet's action, in the absence of any evidence to the contrary, have to abide by his directives."

It goes without saying that it is obligatory upon every Muslim to act publicly and privately in accordance with the spirit of the *Shari'ah* in both peace and war. This caution has to be made because modern military strategies require more vigilance, initiative, and dynamism than those planned and executed in distant times and at different places. This means that the requirements of the present are essentially different from those of the past. If the foregoing instance is considered in this context, it will be clear that purely theoretical but unspecialized and unsystematic reasoning creates false issues and conclusions and tries to resolve the inner contradictions it has created by resorting to hypothetical suppositions.

The very tendency to hunt for textual quotations when considering the nature of the stands and policies to be adopted by the leadership to counter military challenges and resolve political

---

[20] *riddah*: Abjuration of allegiance to Allah as well as to the Islamic state of which one is a citizen.

conflicts is in itself a kind of theoretical thinking which the leadership cannot practically adopt or seriously consider. Objective thinking necessitates approaching and dealing with each problem in the context of its specific requirements in time and place so as to attain clarity of vision about the responsible and unquestionably Islamic reaction demanded by the particular situation.

If we adopt such a realistic and comprehensive approach, there will be no point in making a comparison between the blockade of Banu al Nadir (which occurred at a stage in the foundation of the state in Madīnah when the Muslims were not only outnumbered but also threatened in their very existence by the enemies) and the campaigns by the Muslim army dispatched by Abū Bakr to conquer Iraq and Syria.

The campaign against Banü al Nadir took place at a time when Madīnah had very little power and limited resources. Indeed, the Prophet properly realized that the deterioration of Muslim prestige in Madīnah had made the whole cause vulnerable to the greatest dangers. On the other hand, the Banu al Nadīr, who also enjoyed a well-established solidarity with the Jews, were able to withstand any siege, no matter how long it lasted, because they had a permanent supply of ground water for their orchards in Madīnah on which they very much depended. Madīnah's dates are particularly known for their long-lasting nutritional value. From a military point of view, a prolonged siege was bound to exhaust and incapacitate the Muslim army. Consequently, the Prophet ordered the Muslims to cut down the date trees and burn them in order to reduce the incentive for the Jews to stay in Madīnah and to protect and enjoy their properties. Since date trees take a long time to grow and bear fruit, the Prophet's decision also put an end to the Jew's main source of food. It also ended the conflict in favor of the Muslims without any losses. Realizing the imminent doom that might result from this strategy, Banü al Nadīr requested safe passage out of Madīnah and permission to take with them what they could of their belongings. The true significance of the Prophet's wise strategy was demonstrated by the fact that peace, tranquillity, and prosperity were eventually restored in Madīnah after the forced evacuation of Banü al Nadīr.

Abū Bakr dispatched expeditions to combat the hostile Roman and Persian empires which threatened the very existence of Islam in the Arabian peninsula by stationing some of their military forces along the Muslim borders. These armies practiced all forms of atrocities, especially in Iraq and Syria, where they oppressed the inhabitants, seized their produce and possessions, and prohibited any worship that did not conform to their own faith. Consequently, with proper insight and wisdom, Abū Bakr planned to put an end to this state of violence, tyranny, and oppression in a manner that would not alienate those in whose cause he had dispatched his liberating forces. In other words, he had to act in a manner that would clearly demonstrate the fundamental moral and ethical differences between the Muslims and the non-Muslims. If the liberating armies had been allowed to cut down and burn the date trees, the consequences to the Muslims would have been disastrous. Losing their source of sustenance, the inhabitants would have sided with the old tyrants. Viewed from this angle, the validity and wisdom of Abū Bakr's action cannot be questioned. Both the Prophet's action and that of his successor were appropriate for the particular conditions they faced. There is no point in forcing or permitting a text known to Abū Bakr to raise the issue of deviance from the Prophet's Sunnah. The real problem lies in our approach and in our methods of thinking.

The second example comes from the contemporary *faqih*, Shaykh Sayyid Säbiq, whose writings are very popular in Islamic circles. His book *Fiqh* al Sunnah holds a high place among jurists. The book includes a chapter on jihad wherein this eminent scholar talks about *tabyit* or taking the enemy by night. Sabiq considers various aspects of the subject and elaborates on the reasons that necessitate night attacks, such as fear that the enemy might resort to killing Muslim prisoners of war or totally uninvolved people in case of an open attack. He also considers the negative aspects for the Muslims, such as killing innocent people whom they could not identify in the darkness. He cites many orthodox views on the matter to authenticate and justify his ultimate conclusion that *tabyit* is permissible.

The problem facing the reader who wants to have a full grasp of the subjects of jihad, politics, and war in Islam, however, does not lie in the appropriateness of Sabiq's material or its authentication. It lies, rather, in the failure to satisfy the expectations of the specialist, the research student, the man in authority, and the common reader-each of whom comes to Säbiq's work expecting to find an answer to the challenges he encounters in his special field. Unfortunately, he finds that both the vision and the manner of presentation are disarmingly helpless. Thus, his hopes and expectations are dashed to the ground.

There is no doubt that *tabyit* was an indispensable element in the ancient wars which were fought with swords and spears by soldiers usually on horseback. In those times, though it might have been difficult, it was not impossible to distinguish between one person and another; and should there be any victims, they would not exceed tens or hundreds. But modern wars do not distinguish between day and night, or man and woman. Their victims are counted in the thousands, in fact in the hundreds of thousands. The targets for destruction are chosen according to their strategic significance irrespective of who lives and works there. They can begin and end in the twinkling of an eye. In such wars, the study under discussion is totally irrelevant and useless. The pertinent problem here concerns the method of study, research, presentation, thought, and insight.

If we realize the nature of the problems affecting Islamic thought as a result of its methodological deficiencies, we can easily understand the inadequacy of Islamic political studies. This shortcoming is manifest in the limited, contradictory, and naive nature of our studies despite the loftiness of the principles behind them such as the system of the *khilafah*, *shūra*[21], justice, brotherhood, equality, freedom, and responsibility.

By failing to address important problems, our processes of thought have created chaos in our political perceptions and have made the Ummah incapable of participating actively or exerting

---

[21] *shūra*: The consultative/representational form of government, ordered by Allah (Qur'an 3:159;42:38) and practiced by the Prophet and *al Khulafa' al Rashidün* after him.

sufficient effort to counter the forces that threaten its very existence. There are two types of inadequacies:

1) Misconceptions about original texts and models, which are the source of the Islamic vision that regulates thought and jihad.

2) The perilous, naive, and mindless drive for Westernization, which has caused some of our intellectuals to embrace concepts and systems that have distorted our thought and blurred our vision.

B. *Al Khilafah*: A Case Study in Confusion

One of the most misunderstood concepts in the field of political science is the system of the *khilafah*. Muslim scholars consider it no more than a system of autocracy. Some intellectual leaders even speak apologetically about what they call the just autocrat-*al mustabid al 'adil*. Such tendencies result from the concentration in Islamic studies upon mere technical conditions such as who should be the khalifah, who should be the heir, the pledge of allegiance, the obligation upon the ruler to follow the *Shari'ah*, and the duty of the masses to obey him. But they fail to fathom the core of the political and organizational operation, the factors and forces affecting its structural stability, and the regulations that determine the choice and define the role of the political and social cadres responsible for handing over authority from one leader to another and from one generation to the next. Equally important is the ability of these cadres to supervise the manner of decision-making, the manner in which the leadership exercises authority, and the limits it should not exceed. The urgent need for these fundamental checks and controls totally escapes the attention of the writers in this discipline, due no doubt to the dichotomy between the intellectual and the political leadership and the writers' lack of experience and specialization. These shortcomings have resulted in shallow thinking, unsystematic reasoning, and simplistic perception not only of the systems under consideration but also of history itself.

The misconceptions about the *khilafah* system are not baseless. First, the system holds a tremendous significance in Islamic thought as it vibrates with spiritual as well as historical connotations dating back more than a millennium. As a result of the changes that have taken place since that distant period of time, nostalgic feelings make it difficult, even for an expert, to visualize the workings of the structure of this system.

Needless to say, the study of political systems cannot be confined to studying the official organizations, documents, and regulations of government. It has to include all of the official and unofficial factors and forces that influence the system one way or the other. In the absence of such a comprehensive approach, neither the system nor its working can be understood. Unfortunately, the *khilafah* system does not lend itself to this kind of examination. There is only a bare minimum of officially documented information about the organizational structure of the system. This insufficiency is no fault of the system itself but a natural by-product of the primitive nature of the environment in which it originated. Before the rise of Islam, there was no complex system of monarchy or empire in the Arabian Peninsula. It was inhabited by scattered tribes, each following its own style of life. These tribes had never been united under one government before the establishment of the Muslim society, which, as a result of the challenges it faced and the insufficiency of the human potential, did not pay much attention to the luxury of maintaining codified documents. Therefore, the Muslim government in Madīnah under the rule of the Prophet and his Companions needed to do no more than to lead the Ummah and administer the political and military affairs of the community for twenty-three years. It is no wonder, therefore, that there is a scarcity of detailed information on how leaders were chosen. The Companions who established the government inevitably constituted the collective leadership. They knew about each other's competence and commitment to the cause of Islam. Each of them knew where he stood in relation to the Prophet and the other Companions. This is why the nomination of the khalifah presented no difficulty at all. The mosque provided the place where the cadres of the leadership and the public consulted with each other and settled all matters relating to the welfare of the Ummah. The common commitment to the cause of Islam, which characterized the leaders as well as the members of the public, made the system function smoothly.

The period covered by *al Khulafa' al Rashidūn*, however, was too short for a systematic organization of the foundations on which the transition of the leadership could take place from one generation to the next in accordance with the principles outlined during the life of the Prophet or his immediate successors. This is the reason why immediately after the end of the era of *al Khulafa' al Rashidūn* the fundamental qualities for the choice of a leader, such as seriousness, ability, and religious commitment gave way to tribal bias, self-interest, and power.

Therefore, an examination of the system of *al Khulafa' al Rashidūn* and insight into the manner in which it functioned has to be cautious and specialized. Jumping to shallow conclusions and making sweeping generalizations about concepts such as the benevolent autocrat do more harm than good to the cause of Islam. In addition, such approaches are in direct contradiction to the Qur'an.

This leads me to the conclusion that we have had enough of such irrational inferences. If our concern about our heritage is genuine, we must subject every aspect of that heritage to specialized and systematic study. This is all the more necessary with respect to the modelling of our political set-up on that of *al Khulafa' al Rashidūn.*

One of the issues arising from shortsightedness is the common misconception about the system of *shūrā*. The issue was raised by Abū Bakr's decision during the *riddah* wars. The argument goes that Abū Bakr made the decision to go to war against the *murtadin* in spite of the opposition of 'Umar and some of the other Companions. The strange thing is that those who follow this line of argument cling to marginal points lifted from the text of the dialogue between Abū Bakr, who stood for the war, and the Companions, who argued otherwise.

This argument is faulty because it fails to put the issue in its proper context. It fails to realize that the subjugation of the primitive pagan tribes and their accommodation to the new system occasioned many divine revelations to the Prophet and decisions by him. These show that accepting Islam was one thing, and abiding by the regulations of the new system was quite another. This is expressly stated in the Qur'an (49:14).

Second, this argument fails to appreciate, or rather understand, the character of Abū Bakr, who is known for his tolerance, mercy, compassion, intelligence, and sagacity. In addition, there was nothing novel in the events that led to the *riddah* wars. Even during the life of the Prophet some tribes revolted against the new system and some individuals even claimed prophethood. Names such as Musaylamah, Sajjah, and al Aswad al Anasi are well known. Well aware of this background, Abū Bakr would never have made an immature or a thoughtless decision. Those who think otherwise fail to realize the amount of time and the degree of effort needed to fathom the subtle considerations that underlie important political decisions.

A comprehensive examination of the issue reveals that it was much more than a theoretical confrontation or a quibble about words, as the available studies we have want us to believe. First, the issue poses important questions about the social and political reorganization of the Arabian Peninsula under a new system. Second, the issue here provides a concrete example of the problems that influence political decisions and the conditions that underline the responsibility of accepting political leadership. This is clearly shown in the confrontation between Abū Bakr as khalifah and 'Umar as a representative of a group that did not at first understand the magnitude of the issue. 'Umar told Abu Bakr that he should either accept the opinion of his counselors or leave the *khilafah*. Abū Bakr did not accept either of these alternatives. He stuck to his opinion with the full conviction that he was doing the right thing and argued patiently and persuasively in favor of his opinion. Eventually 'Umar and his supporters were able to perceive and concede to Abū Bakr's viewpoint. 'Umar later admitted that Abū Bakr's perseverance, subtle firmness, and acute intelligence left no ground for misunderstanding or ambiguity. The force of the argument opened the hearts of his opponents to the truth of his convictions, and they consequently reconciled themselves to the right path. This issue amply demonstrates that the khalifah had no authority over his counselors, but it was his personal characteristics which won him their support and full confidence. It is pertinent to mention here that they had previously told the khalifah that if they observed in him any deviation from the right path, they would straighten him out by the use of force. Their acquiescence in this particular case shows their conviction of and satisfaction with Abū Bakr's point of view.

The objective researcher will not fail to realize the significance of *shūra* and how it was practiced during the period of *al Khulafa' al Rashidūn*. Mutual consultation was the rule rather than the exception. There was no place for any form of despotism. Those who think otherwise are definitely short-sighted. Their failure lies in their inability to distinguish between executive and administrative matters which necessarily limit the scope of responsibility, and major political decisions which require consultation, the exchange of ideas, and a minute examination of these ideas so that the final decision will be binding on all concerned because of their conviction and satisfaction. Such consultation and conviction are essential to success.

C. Un-Islamic Concepts and Terminology

There is a great deal of confusion in Islamic studies regarding foreign systems and the political terminology used in them. This confusion is due to the researchers' insufficient knowledge of the foreign systems on the one hand and the inadequacy of their approach on the other. These drawbacks are further augmented by thoughtlessly striving to catch up with the standards of the so-called civilized world. Under such pressure, research is hastily conducted and consequently not only fails to achieve the desired goals but also adds to the confusion, lack of discrimination, and uncertainty.

1. Democracy

The two related concepts of democracy and sovereignty are alien to our culture. Nonetheless, Muslim scholars have given them undue importance both as academic terms and as concepts. Some scholars go so far as to argue that they are in tune with the spirit and teachings of Islam and have to be adopted into Islamic thought and political systems.

There is no doubt that there are some apparent similarities between these concepts and the overall spirit of Islam. Unfortunately, these concepts contain un-Islamic elements which our scholars have failed to detect. Through this failure, Islamic thought has inherited a kaleidoscopic phenomenon in which the pursuit of insignificant similarities has brought about undesirable notions that completely distort an already blurred vision.

Democracy, both as a concept and a system, has ancient roots in Western history, thought, and philosophy. It does not signify merely the procedural measures of choosing political leaders; it is a natural extension of the materialistic philosophy that regards man as a physical entity whose value is measured in terms of the pragmatic or utilitarian sense of his usefulness to the state, society, and the world. The spiritual aspect of man's existence, which is his real value, is not stressed in this system. In essence, democracy is no more than an amalgamation of individuals who, by forming a majority, assume the right and the power to propagate their thoughts and achieve their personal interests, while making minimal concessions to minorities.

This is the reason why concepts such as majority, minority, election, party system, etc., are of paramount importance in Western political systems. Since these systems are based on secular foundations, any concept of justice cannot be of real value to the individual or society. Indeed, the systems provide legal loopholes for the strong to gratify their personal interests at the expense of the weak.

Although *shūrā* aims at choosing the proper leadership, establishing checks and controls over them, and arriving at decisions accepted, appreciated, and supported by the public, it is not the same thing as democracy, which seemingly seeks to achieve similar purposes. By definition, *shūrā* derives from a philosophical perception essentially different from that of democracy. This difference lies in the notion of justice as a concrete fact of existence which man arrives at through his own nature and divine revelation, and which he endeavors to attain irrespective of his personal desires and interests. As a method, the system of *shūrā* provides the procedure whereby Muslims sit together and deliberate upon important matters to arrive at and be bound by conclusions in the light of the philosophical concept of justice. If the issue under consideration does not concern justice but is a case of preferring one to the other, there is no harm in adopting measures such as voting, abiding by the point of view of the minority, etc. The same measures could be resorted to if the discussion reached a deadlock in the absence of an authentic analogy. But even here, no decision should be taken until everybody has had the chance to express his or her opinion and cite relevant evidence.

Hasty decisions, insufficient investigation, and blind imitation will not bring about the reform we desire. If we concentrate on the philosophical background of the concepts pertaining to this or that system, we will be able to develop insight into the nature of Islamic political systems, whose processes for arriving at and executing decisions are totally different from those of the West. Blind Westernization will not only cause us to drift away from our avowed goals but will ultimately lead to catastrophic results.

2) Sovereignty

Some Muslim scholars have introduced the concept of sovereignty into Islamic thought, arguing that the pledge of loyalty by individual persons to the *khalifah* confers sovereignty on the *Ummah*. Others disagree with this view on the grounds that since divinely revealed knowledge is the only source of the *Shari'ah*, no mortal can be vested with such powers. Thus, the term sovereignty applies to Allah alone. In my opinion, any debate on the merits or demerits of this term with the intention of adopting or rejecting it does no service to Islamic thought. It distorts rather than clarifies the vision.

Sovereignty is a Western concept deeply rooted in the gradual evolution of Western systems. On all occasions it was resorted to in order to determine who should be entrusted with the responsibility of decision-making in the fields of politics and legislation. It first emerged during the confrontation between the monarchy and the feudal lords who gained power by uniting during the emergence of the European nationalist states. Eventually, the term sovereignty was used to indicate the placing of political and legislative power in the hands of the representatives of the people. This became politically evident after the broadening of political participation and the emergence of new classes which sought to achieve positions of influence within the competing industrial and commercial communities.

Arguments about adopting or rejecting this term clearly show not only an insufficient awareness of the nature of the Islamic constitution but also an inability to distinguish between the varying levels of decision-making in Islamic systems. It is incorrect to assume that any one authority or level of authority in the legislative affairs of the Ummah is absolute. Nor is it correct to assume that legislative bodies do not exist in the Muslim Ummah. To dispel any misconceptions in this regard, we have to be aware of the different legislative levels on the basis of which we can determine the fields of specialization in Muslim communities. The basic constitutional elements, which are the fundamental principles and values revealed in the Qur'an, cannot be questioned or tampered with; they must be accepted as they are. But legislation at the level of the daily concerns of existence and to which we do not find any direct reference in the Qur'an, or the Sunnah can be handled by the specialist bodies in the various sectors of the Ummah. If we reject this, how can we possibly explain Islamic practices such as *ijtihad*, *ra'i* (opinion) and *tarjih* (preponderance)? If the outcome of such efforts is not called "legislation," what else can we call it? In practice, many of our differences and disputes are settled through the previously mentioned channels which neither permit confrontation over the source of the decision taken nor cause enmity between the deliberating parties. There is no place for victory or defeat.

Blind imitation of Western systems ultimately leads to confusion in defining the spheres within which the various bodies conducting the affairs of the Ummah should behave in accordance with Islamic teachings. Mixing the two systems by adopting the concept of sovereignty leads either to depriving the *Ummah* of the power of decision-making and turning it over to an individual who behaves according to his own personal interpretation of what is right and wrong, or placing absolute authority in the hands of the Ummah irrespective of whether the structure is compatible with the spirit of Islam.

Sovereignty has no place in the framework in which the Islamic political structure is organized, but it does exist in the workings of the basic legislative spheres. The issue posed is not whether the source of decision-making is revealed knowledge or the Ummah. The real issue needed for the implementation of a properly Islamic system is a method which enables the *Ummah* to practice its role and authority in accordance with the true purpose and spirit of Islamic teachings. This method is necessary to understand properly the nature of the Islamic framework, its evolution, and the challenges it has encountered since the *Umawiyun* period, as well as to sustain a commitment to its future.

3) Separation of Church and State

In the absence of a clear-cut Islamic literature in the field of political science, Muslim scholars continue to pose the question whether Islam is a state, a religion, or both. This debate entails feelings of embarrassment in Muslim scholars whenever there is a call for the restoration of the *khilafah* in our age. These two issues amply demonstrate the success of orientalists and hostile non-Muslims in confusing and misleading the thought of scholars.

By raising these issues, our attention has been diverted from more useful engagements. Indeed, in the absence of a proper method and research, we will never attain any clarity of vision and will continue to mistake trivial issues for important ones. Comprehensive insight into Islam reveals that it does not sanction any form of separation between religion and politics. Islam signifies that concepts such as the nature of the Creator, good and evil, the Hereafter, etc., all aim at giving proper guidance to man's behavior at the individual as well as at the social levels. This point is too obvious to be elaborated upon. But the fact remains that there are conditions which have resulted in unnecessarily prolonged and futile discussions on the preceding themes. These conditions are: the non-Muslims' distorted picture of Christianity; Muslim awareness of the crisis of knowledge; and Muslim dissatisfaction with the existing systems and an urgent desire to find an easy way out of the crisis. Thus, enemies of Islam were able to take advantage of this situation by writing about Islam in a manner that would make the non-perceptive Muslim believe that they were praising it. They would glorify it as a legacy full of indisputable divine secrets that ignore the social needs of human existence. Once that un-Islamic idea had been inculcated, they began to hammer the minds of Muslims with concepts such as racism, nationalism, secularism, and communism-all of which are contrary to the purposes, principles, and values of Islam. The end result for the Muslims is confusion, decadence, and incapacity.

The issue of the *khilafah* is representative of a state of confusion among Muslims over Islamic ideals, values, principles, and their historical application in Muslim societies.

Generally, it is extremely difficult if not impossible to reinstitute historical systems in their entirety. This makes the hope of reestablishing the *khilafah* system only a remote possibility, especially if the system is interpreted as a practical embodiment of political organizations. This is true whether such hopes are entertained by Orientalists or Muslim scholars, irrespective of the degree of accurate perception in such interpretations. It needs to be emphasized that the *khilafah* is no more than an Islamic term denoting the establishment of a social and political system in Islam. Any system, whatever its form, based on the requirements of time and place, can be in keeping with the *khilafah* system provided that it adheres to the Islamic fundamentals regulating the spiritual and mundane affairs of the Ummah. No true Muslim would accept a system that is not based upon and committed to that Islamic purpose.

The *khilafah* system is an ideal for which every Muslim must strive. But our struggle should not be clouded by transcendental or historical misconceptions. Nor should we be misled by those who have no respect for our Islamic identity. Such efforts require perseverance, determination, and originality.

D. Political Studies in Muslim Universities

The main theme of this essay is the need for the Islamization of knowledge in general and that of political science in particular. The first prerequisite in the process of Islamization is to have a clear idea of the reality of Islamic political studies. Without going into details, one could say that texts pertaining to Islamic political studies are no more than a handful of personal reflections on Islamic constitutional law, administration, biographies, and laws regulating war and peace. Despite that narrow scope, or perhaps because of it, they occupy a marginal place in most academic curricula. These studies are insufficient because:

1) There are scarcely any analytical studies in the field of Islamic political thought;

2) There is no effort to trace the nature and significance of issues brought about by political phenomena in Islamic history;

3) There is no attempt to distinguish between original and alien elements, or permanent and ephemeral elements, in the system;

4) There is no clear-cut Islamic definition of international relations;

5) The historical factors that actually influenced the foundations of the Ummah, its experiences, and interactions with other nations have been totally ignored;

6) The studies conducted both locally and internationally about Islamic systems of government and the lessons to be learnt from the actual application of these systems are also inadequate.

The reforms we are striving to achieve require the Islamization of knowledge in general and that of political science in particular, because without proper insight into this field the reconstruction of the Ummah and the preparation of cadres for leadership are impossible. Initially, this can be done by founding research centres and holding discussions in the hope of clarifying our vision and defining our objectives on a more systematic basis. Those in charge of such activities should be specialists committed to the cause of Islam and to the welfare of the *Ummah*. Admittedly, the effort needed can be exacting, because it requires the comprehensive and systematic analysis of the legacy of Islam in all its primary and secondary sources. A great deal of editing will be needed. Subjects will have to be categorized; terms will have to be coined, modified, or defined anew. A total renovation will be required.

Armed with deep insight, critical understanding, and systematic analysis, we would not refrain from investigating knowledge discovered by non-Muslims or adopting new experimental methods, provided that we remain conscious of the differences in background, motivation, and purpose.

A great deal of time has already been wasted. Research centres and academic institutes should now take up the challenge.

www.ingramcontent.com/pod-product-compliance
Ingram Content Group UK Ltd.
Pitfield, Milton Keynes, MK11 3LW, UK
UKHW021410190726
13845UKWH00028B/1002

9 788119 946488